Now the Green Blade Rises

Also by Elizabeth Spires

POETRY

Worldling (1995)
Annonciade (1989)
Swan's Island (1985)
Globe (1981)

FOR CHILDREN

I Am Arachne (2001)
The Mouse of Amherst (1999)
Riddle Road (1999)
With One White Wing (1995)

EDITED BY ELIZABETH SPIRES

The Instant of Knowing: Lectures,
    Criticism, and Occasional Prose
    of Josephine Jacobsen (1997)

Now the Green Blade Rises

Elizabeth Spires

W. W. Norton & Company
New York   London

For information about permission to reproduce selections from this book,
write to Permissions, W. W. Norton & Company, Inc.,
500 Fifth Avenue, New York, NY 10110

The text of this book is composed in Goudy with the display set in Pouty
Composition by Gina Webster
Manufacturing by The Courier Companies, Inc.
Book design by Charlotte Staub
Production manager: Amanda Morrison

Library of Congress Cataloging-in-Publication Data
Spires, Elizabeth.
    Now the green blade rises / Elizabeth Spires.
        p. cm.
    ISBN 0-393-05146-3
    I. Title.
PS3569.P554 N69 2002
813'.54—dc21   2002023570

W. W. Norton & Company, Inc., 500 Fifth Avenue,
New York, N.Y. 10110
www.wwnorton.com

W. W. Norton & Company Ltd., Castle House, 75/76 Wells Street,
London W1T 3QT

1 2 3 4 5 6 7 8 9 0

IN MEMORY OF MY MOTHER

Elizabeth Sue Spires

1931–1998

Now the green blade rises from the buried grain,
Wheat that in the dark earth many days has lain;
Love lives again that with the dead has been;
Love is come again like wheat arising green.

—FROM A CAROL BY JOHN M. C. CRUM

Contents

The Cabin 13

I Dogwood 17
Reprieve, Reprise 19
Cemetery Reef 21
White Curtain 23
Ghazal 25
Riddle 26
My Mother's Doll 27
"Chapel in the Woods" 29
Anamnesis 31
Now the Green Blade Rises 33

II Two Chairs on a Hillside 37
Infant Joy 40
The Rose 42
The Faces of Children 43
The Daughter of Snow 44
Flight Back 45
I Dreamed a Dream 46
The Frame 48
Like Water 49
1999 50
The Beautiful Day 52

III Above the Pagoda 57

Two Characters in Search of a Metaphor 59

The Papermaker 61

Bruise 63

Silence 65

Grass 66

Triptych for Three Tenses 67

Curio 68

Rocko 70

A Dream of Water 72

"In Heaven It Is Always Autumn" 73

Notes and Dedications 75

Acknowledgments

The poems in this book first appeared in the following magazines:

Agni Review: "The Daughter of Snow"

American Poetry Review: "The Cabin"; "1999"

Atlanta Review: "A Dream of Water"

Image: "Now the Green Blade Rises"; " 'Chapel in the Woods'"

Kenyon Review: "Two Chairs on a Hillside"; "I Dreamed a Dream"

The New Criterion: "Dogwood"; "Reprieve, Reprise"; "White Curtain"; "Grass"; "Above the Pagoda"; "Triptych for Three Tenses"; "Curio"; " 'In Heaven It Is Always Autumn'"; "Like Water"

New England Review: "Anamnesis"; "Silence"; "The Faces of Children"

The New Yorker: "The Rose"

Partisan Review: "The Frame"

Pequod: "The Papermaker"

Ploughshares: "Ghazal"; "Infant Joy"

Poetry: "Cemetery Reef"; "Bruise"; "Two Characters in Search of a Metaphor"

Southwest Review: "Riddle"

"Dogwood," "Cemetery Reef," and " 'In Heaven It Is Always Autumn'" appeared in *Contemporary American Poetry*, 7th Edition, edited by Al Poulin Jr. and Michael Waters (Houghton Mifflin, 2000).

"Two Chairs on a Hillside," "1999," and " 'In Heaven It Is Always Autumn'" appeared in *The New Bread Loaf Anthology of*

Contemporary American Poetry, edited by Michael Collier and Stanley Plumly (Middlebury College Press, 1999).

The author would like to thank the Whiting Foundation, the American Academy of Arts and Letters, and Goucher College for their support during the writing of these poems.

Now the Green Blade Rises

The Cabin

Robert Frost's cabin; Ripton, Vermont

The two-lane highway rushes up and down,
a white line down its middle leading it on.
It curves the way the stream beside it curves,
carved out by glaciers in a time when the world was ice.
Past time is with you always, always here.
It's held in gorge and meadow, in grey-green moss,
in lichens, in boulderspill from old stone walls.
So turn at the wayside onto an unmarked road
that leads a mile uphill, then dwindles to a grassy path
though August woods, dim as a church and cool.
A fallen birch will block your path. You'll hear
him saying clearly (you who imagine such things):
You can't go farther! Can't go in my woods!
Ignore the warning and press on to find his cabin
in a clearing, its door locked to the world.
With the right key, the door will open to you,
you who are neither first nor last to come here,
why have you come? To crank the old black phone
in the kitchen, hoping a voice at the end of the line
might answer? To idly turn the pencil sharpener,
the kind he used in a schoolroom when he was master,
its silver blade sharpening the point of all he said?
Here, in the bare front room, a lapboard on his lap,
he wrote about the weather outside and in his head.
Nothing betrays him except, half-hidden on the mantel,
a chipped toy goblet, rose-red when the light shines on it,
something a child might play with, a child long gone.
Now take down the book of letters from the shelf
that opens on its own to his words after a daughter's death:

We thought to move heaven and earth—heaven with prayers
and earth with money. We moved nothing. And here we are,
Cadmus and Harmonia, not yet placed safely in changed forms.
Somewhere beyond these rooms, these trees, this path,
he's laughing his dark laugh, changed the way the wood
in the woodpile changes, softening over years so slowly
the eye can't see, unless the eye has all eternity.
When you leave, leave all as it was—the black phone
on the hook, the heavy book back on the shelf—
for the next one who comes as curiously as you did.
Outside, linger for a moment. Sit on the old stone slab
he raised up off the ground and made into a bench
(the kind that, lettered, might mark a grave).
Stare at the mountain that was his constant companion.
It looks at you without emotion, it does not rage or love,
as he did, and yet its permanence consoles. The wind
is picking up, moving the trees to softly whisper, *Ssshhh!*
A spider on your shoe is listening to all you say.

I

*I do not recognize memory in the sense in which
you mean it. Whatever we encounter that is great,
beautiful, significant, need not be remembered from
outside, need not be hunted up and laid hold of as it
were. Rather, from the beginning, it must be woven
into the fabric of our inmost self, must become one
with it, create a new and better self in us and thus
live and become a productive force in ourselves.
There is no past that one is allowed to long for.
There is only the eternally new, growing from the
enlarged elements of the past; and genuine longing
always must be productive, must create something
new and better.*

—GOETHE

Dogwood

Whiter than paper, whiter than snow,
whiter than the moon in its fullness,
whiter than clouds passing over,

> *I close my eyes and see white stars*
> *hanging in the air of the backyard.*
> *For weeks they are out there.*

Whiter than music, whiter than bone,
whiter than ivory, whiter than hope,
whiter than prayer, whiter than a name,

> *Whitest of all white things in the world,*
> *I want to know what you know.*

Whiter than silence, whiter than thought,
whiter than interruption, whiter than frost,
whiter than the body's hollows,

> *Now, after too many white words,*
> *I stumble and touch branches heavy*
> *with ten thousand blurred white petals.*

Whiter than love or death,
whiter than my winter breath,
whiter than a white room's emptiness,

> *As if I could count them all, one*
> *for each man, woman and child.*

Whiter than the blank white sky,
whiter than the white of an eye,
whiter than foam on the breaking black wave—

For weeks you have stood there,
arms raised like a priest
in silent ceremony, praising creation

in the only way you know,
now tell me why we have to die.

Reprieve, Reprise

*After the lord of the dark world carried her away, she was never again
the gay young creature who had played in the flowery meadow without
a thought of care or trouble. She did indeed rise from the dead every
spring, but she brought with her the memory of where she had come
from; with all her bright beauty, there was something strange and
awesome about her. She was often said to be "the maiden whose name
may not be spoken."*   —EDITH HAMILTON, *Mythology*

Mother, I had a vision of you:
in what distant future did I see
your body shrouded in light,
jeweled and dusted in light?

A premonition, I thought,
of a future I'd have no part of,
where death overtook love
and love was powerless

to draw the loved one back.
For years I never spoke of it,
but now you lie in a room
that is not a room,

neither crypt nor tomb,
your body mapped with lines
and X's that guide the X-ray light
to seek out what is dark, malign.

A door closes between us,
and I see you captured
on a screen, in still repose:
my vision carried all these years!

A hand twirls a dial, a whir
for a few brief seconds as light
pierces through you, then silence.
With a click, the door opens

and you are given back—
you pass back through the door!—
something the dead cannot do
so I know you cannot be dead.

You return, as once a daughter
passed from a dark underworld
back into her mother's arms
(but I am daughter here, not you),

how gratefully she passed back.
I see them standing in a field
at noon, the light too bright
to bear, no shadows anywhere.

What do they hear? They hear
the birds, the wind, the brook.
And Nature says what it always
says, what always remains unheard:

Happiness is fleet. Like water running
over stones, the words repeat:
Happiness is fleet, is fleet, is fleet . . .
Or do they imagine it so?

Cemetery Reef

Grand Cayman Island

Walking down the beach, I took your arm.
The treatments were over. Your hair was growing back.
For a week, time lay suspended. And yet, too fast,
too soon, everything was changing to memory.
But your arm was real when I touched it, real flesh and blood.
We were talking about doctors when I saw the blowfish,
green as the greenest apple, puffed-up and bobbing
    in the shallows.
But when I looked again, it was only a pair of bathing trunks,
ballooning out, aimlessly knocked back and forth by the tide.
Ahead, the cruise ships lay at anchor in the harbor.
At noon they'd slip away, like days we couldn't hold onto,
dropping over the blurred blue horizon to other ports of call.
The hotels we were passing all looked out to water,
a thousand beach chairs in the sand looked out to water,
but no one sat there early in the morning. And no one
slept in the empty hammock at the Governor's House
where workmen in grey coveralls raked the seaweed
    into piles,
until the sand was white and smooth, like paper not yet
    written on.

All lies in retrospect now: how, each afternoon,
we put on masks and fins and swam to Cemetery Reef.
The coral looked like brains and flowers, like unreal cities
of melted peaks and towers, pointing up to where the sun,
flat and round as a host, lay dissolving on the water.
Schools of fish, bright as neon, ragged as flags,
drifted directionless with the tide, or swerved

and hid from our reaching hands in beds of waving kelp.
We breathed through snorkels, did the dead man's float,
the hollow rushing sound we heard inside our heads
our own frail breath going slowly *in* and *out*. Farther out,
the shallow reef dropped off to chasm, the waves
choppy and thick, the calm clear water darkening to ink.
How far could we swim before exhaustion took us,
before a shark or barracuda rounded a cornerless corner
to meet us eye to eye? My mind circled back to our dinner
in the Chinese restaurant: the waiter bringing six cookies
on a plate, alike in every way, except that one, just one,
contained a different fate. *Wealth, long life, happiness,*
the plate was passed around. Then your turn came.
You chose one, broke it open, read aloud,
Soon you will cross the great water, dropping it, as if stung.

And then, too quickly, it was the last day.
Dreaming, we all came to. We were back at Cemetery Reef,
walking a narrow path of broken shells toward
    the shining water.
Off to one side, a low stone wall squared off the cemetery,
the dead buried aboveground in white weathered slabs,
their plots neatly surrounded by smooth white stones.
Morning of all mornings, you swam out to the reef alone,
came back. Gathering our things to go, what made me say,
When we come back. . . . All lies unanswered now.
I remember how the flowers on the graves were red
and white plastic, the color of flesh and blood, of regret,
of paper not yet written on. Put there, *In Memory.*
In a colder place, we would soon—unwilling, stunned—
remember you with the kind that always die.

White Curtain

Late that afternoon, I lay
on the bed, the wind
blowing through the room.
It was fall, the days gold.

The white curtain, sheer
as a soul, lifting in the wind.
As if a hand, unthinking hand,
disturbed its calm repose.

It fluttered and rose.
Fluttered and rose.
Or did it twist in mortal
agony? I didn't know.

Unceasing flow!
The everlasting present
passing, forever passing,
through our lives,

the drift and pull of pain
remembered, my name
called out in a dream,
and the question,

Mother, where are you?
The wind saying everything,
nothing that I didn't already
know: *She is dying.*

Light. Tears. Breath. Wind.
I watched and could do
nothing as the curtain
rose and fell.

Ghazal

My name in the black air, called out in the early morning.
A premonition dreamed: waking, I beheld a future of mourning.

Our partings were rehearsals for the final scene: you and I
in a desert, saying goodbye on a white September morning.

The call came. West, I flew west again. Impossible, but the sun
didn't move. I stepped off the plane and it was still morning.

I've always worn black. Now a blank whiteness outlines
everything. What shall I put on this loneliest of mornings?

You've left an envelope. Inside, your black pearl earrings
and a note: *Your grandmother's. Good.* In ink the color
    of mourning.

I remember the songs you used to sing. Blue morning glories
    on the vine.
An owl in the tree of heaven. All of my childhood's
    sacred mornings.

Your mother before you. Her mother before her. I, before
    my daughter.
It's simple, I hear you explain. *We are all daughters in mourning.*

I was your namesake, a firstborn *Elizabeth* entering
the world on a May morning. I cannot go back to that morning.

Riddle

What you were and were not:
I was. Both you and not you.
I grew by taking from you.

Once, years ago, the scrim
parted: we were in the car,
smoke from your cigarette

spiralling round you,
and I, a child, saw you
for a moment as someone

unfamiliar, apart
from me, as I might see
a stranger on the street.

Older, I looked at you
and saw myself, saw more
than I was prepared to see.

Our last best selves survive.
They shine in a dim place,
and I am more and less

than what I was,
the riddle now not
who you were, Mother,

but what am I?

My Mother's Doll

After she died, I found you slumped in the living room
where she kept you, a rag doll, tall as I was,
made years ago by my grandmother.
You stared straight ahead, your mouth
a thin unsmiling line, one fingerless hand
flopped across your chest. Dark secret keeper,
big sister in pain, you used to amuse us with your mood,
making perpetual despair look easy as you sat,
mute and gloomy as a cloud, listening to all that we said.

When I closed up her apartment, I propped you up
in the straightback chair but wondered later—
at home in my own bed—if it was the right thing to do.
I imagined you sitting in darkness all winter,
the blinds drawn, only the dust to keep you company.
Did your heart beat faster when you heard the hum
of the refrigerator? When a letter fell through the mail slot?
Or did you lapse into a sleep deeper than my own,
cold, dark, profound, where winter passed in a dream
and you, in your solitude, were nothing, *no one*,
because she wasn't there to speak your name?

Coming back this summer, I open the blinds
and let light stream into the room.
Dust motes swirl without meaning in the air.
Outside the pear tree is in bloom,
but you don't turn your head.
I pick you up and hold you in my arms.
Then eye to eye, I waltz you around the room
to make my daughter laugh, my daughter

who barely knew my mother.
When we leave, I'll straighten your blue dress,
comb your mop of hair into a neat page boy.
Then I'll put you back into the chair until the next time
because I cannot imagine it empty,
cannot imagine this room without you.

"Chapel in the Woods"

a sign nailed to a tree in the countryside

I found a chapel in the woods, bare and spare
as love or grief, where a pine tree, tall
as a roof beam, branched out to shelter open air,

the tamped-down, unswept floor littered
with pine needles from the passing years.
Stone balanced on stone to make a pulpit

a Sunday preacher might grip in exhortation,
a leafy backdrop changing as the seasons
changed, going from green to gold to white.

Pansies, white, pink, and darker pink,
grew in unspoiled clusters among tufts
of grass, their faces upturned to the sun.

I knelt down and picked three
to press into the pages of a book.
Then I sat for a while on a fallen log,

the sun slanting through the trees the way
it does in late fall, warming one cheek,
leaving the other in shadow, and I thought

of two hands, one young, one old,
one warm, one cool, clasping each other,
clasping each other, then letting go.

Suddenly a wind came up to warn
that all would change. Crows called
back and forth. Clouds raced across the sky,

headed toward a final, unknown
destination. I was alone. Or was I?
In the underbrush, I heard the rustle

of leaves, the snap of a twig breaking,
heavy footfalls. Then the afternoon was over,
a deer breaking cover, running free.

Anamnesis

When we meet again without our bodies,
meet in the grave's cold bed,
when, fingerbone to fingerbone,
we touch, will time be frozen forever,
or run on as it always has,
a stream neither fast nor slow?

When, our faces gone, we speak
through the softness of moss,
through crumbling moss-soft lips,
will our words unsay themselves,
or will our voices meet again
in rising recognition?

When, like the blind, we search
for our names in the tomb's shadow,
will we find them lost forever,
or will our anxious fingers touch
the upraised edge of letters chiseled
in stone? Tell me if you know.

Once, I apprehended All:
I saw light streaming through stone,
and you in the sere clothes of the dead.
A fine dust lay on everything. You said
not one word. How could you?
I did not touch you then.

It is only a matter of time
before I lie down beside you

and we become all things to each other—
mother, child, thief, betrayer, love, friend—
we will be all things as we whisper,
How green life was!

Now the Green Blade Rises

italicized lines from a carol by John M. C. Crum

Sometimes, when the phone
rings, I think it is you.
Three months, and I still believe
I'll hear your voice at the other end
of the line. But you're dead,
and the world is ash. *Your body.*
Words that used to live.

I had a dream, black and pictureless.
You were calling my name
over a great distance. It hung
suspended in the dark air,
but I could not move,
had no voice to answer.
Mother, forgive me if you can.

Now, if I could, I would sit
with you in a simple pew
somewhere quiet and dim.
To be there would be enough.
There'd be nothing we'd have to say.
The moment, held like a book
between us, a silent offering.

It would be midwinter.
We'd watch the slant light
of late afternoon stream
through high windows
to warm cool stones, warm us,

and fall on an open hymnal
to lines we'd read by touch:

> *Now the green blade rises from the buried grain,*
> *Wheat that in the dark earth many days has lain;*
> *Love lives again that with the dead has been;*
> *Love is come again like wheat arising green.*

There, soul to soul,
we would have forever
to finally speak again.

II

Two Chairs on a Hillside

"Look up. And tell me what you see."

> "I see two chairs on a hillside.
> What are they doing there?"

"Through good days and bad, two sat there
having a conversation. Flowers grew up around them,
vines twined around their chairs. They didn't seem to care,
but moved the chairs higher or lower to adjust the view
of rushing streams and valleys, a town that they both knew.
Autumn approached, the hillside changing color,
and still they stayed, feeling the change within themselves.
Their talk was a thread unspooling, leading them where
    it would.
Sometimes one lost the thread, her mind for a moment blank,
and then she'd find herself, again pick up the thread.
With the first chill wind, their bare hands touched,
as if to reassure. They braced themselves, pulling their coats
closer, as snow fell through the air, whitening all they said."

> "And so they stayed all winter?"

"They did. Shivering and skeletal, they preferred frost
to interruption. They wintered out the worst with words
until their rags thawed out. Spring came again.
Green shoots, some from the heart, sprang up.
They felt themselves anew. Each had a story to tell.
The first recalled an island where summer lasted
year to year. South, she flew south, pulled by a dream
of herself unlike the northern dream she knew.
Like the first face one sees on waking, she loved that place.

One year she lost its whereabouts, the next, that face,
and suddenly she found herself alone and ancient
on a hillside looking down. The view inspired a poem.
The second came up and found her there, white pages
blowing down the hillside. Each was surprised
to find a compatriot. That's how it all began."

"And the second?"

"The second is harder to speak of.
She moved in extremes of ice and fire,
swinging from hate to love. Her passion
took her up the hillside, away from the town.
Once there, she would have liked to stay,
climbing higher than mid-range. I can't say
more than that. That's all that I can say."

"Don't then. You've said enough."

"Have I? I've only told part of it.
You've heard how poets stand in fields and pray
for lightning on the bluest day? They never had.
They weren't that crazy. And yet, one day it struck
between them, the ground parting for an instant,
then closing up, taking the first somewhere dark.
The second wasn't surprised, and yet she was.
She sat there grieving, stunned. As some will talk
to a grave, she talked to the chair's vacancy,
believing she was heard—"

"Perhaps she was."

"—Then she came down to where we're standing.
She stood where I stand now. Stars wheeled
around her, the night sky streamed and blurred,
the scene seen as if through tears. Then all was quiet,
the sky as fixed and deep and measureless as before.
Each night I stand here looking up. The chairs are proof
of what I've told you. Can you see them up there?
Two empty chairs no element can change, as fixed
in their relation as any starry constellation—"

                    "As we are?"

"No, as we will be someday. We aren't complete
in what we are yet. We're in the middle of a story
we'll tell twice over, each in our own slant way.
We've written half the pages, but half remain.
To be done, if at all, out of love—"

                    "How do you know all this?
                    Who told you?"

"I was one of the two."

Infant Joy

L. infantia, *inability to speak*

I hear your infant voice again,
unspooling on a tape made years ago—
No, though it was paradise, I can't,

can't go back to that room, filled
with the rounded vowels, the sighs
and crooning of a newborn child,

bright syllables strung, like beads
on a string, into meaningless meaning.
One night, as you slept,

I read Blake's song:
I have no name:
I am but two days old.

By a circle of light, I read,
exhausted, stunned:
What shall I call thee?

And you, in a dream
beyond me, cried out:
I happy am, Joy is my name.

You laughed the laugh of creation.
Beyond the darkened room,
a framing radiance. Beyond

the framing radiance, the world.
But for an everlasting moment,
we were there, *together*,

in a place such as Blake knew,
your infant syllables dissolving terror,
fear, all that could befall me, you.

Meaningless meaning made new!
Sweet joy but two days old,
Sweet joy I call thee . . .

And I was laughing, too,
to read Blake's song.

The Rose

We waited for the roses to bloom.
They were your flower. Always in my mind,
your face on the first day, a tightly folded rose.
But the roses were a month away.

There, on the lawn, you moved from isle
to lit isle, choosing the tulip, the daffodil,
the dandelion. You made no distinction.
Everything was yours for the taking,

the pale wisteria, a bloom off the dogwood,
diffuse and free and calm as a mind
that spends itself completely on its blossoming.
You forgot me. You left me behind,

stepping in and out of shadow, as if the grass
were water, the pooling light a stepping-stone.
Quick-footed, sure, never for a moment
would you be lost in a rushing stream of years.

And then, hands full of flowers,
how easily you ran back to where I stood—
O, I stood in a place different from you—
and said, *These are for you* . . .

I stared at you over a great chasm of time
as, over and over, you brought me spring flowers.

The Faces of Children

Meeting old friends after a long time, we see
with surprise how they have changed, and must imagine,
despite the mirror's lies, that change is upon us, too.

Once, in our twenties, we thought we would never die.
Now, as one thoughtlessly shuffles a deck of cards,
we have run through half our lives.

The afternoon has vanished, the evening changing
us into four shadows mildly talking on a porch.
And as we talk, we listen to the children play

the games that we played once. In joy and terror,
they cry out in surprise as the seeker finds the one in hiding,
or, in fairytale tableau, each one is tapped and turned

to stone. The lawn is full of breathing statues who wait
to be changed back again, and we can do nothing but stand
to one side of our children's games, our children's lives.

We are the conjurors who take away all pain,
and we are the ones who cannot take away the pain at all.
They do not ask, as lately we have asked ourselves,

Who was I then? And what must I become?
Like newly minted coins, their faces catch
the evening's radiance. They are so sure of us,

more sure than we are of ourselves. Our children:
who gently push us toward the end of our own lives.
The future beckons brightly. They trust us to lead them there.

The Daughter of Snow

To stand in a white dress,
the work of a winter afternoon,
eyes a pair of sky-blue marbles,
mouth a line of twisted yarn,
arms two outstretched branching twigs,
the world made blue by what you are . . .

To stand very still and not
to cry out as the afternoon darkens,
and the ground steams, and the sound
of running snowmelt breaks the silence.
To feel the passing of things you cannot
touch that touch you with their being . . .

Now as my daughter sleeps,
I kneel down to what you are,
knowing you will be gone tomorrow.
May your heart that is not there,
the white heart of the snow,
be my heart, too.

Flight Back

for my sister

Flying west to east, I carried the roses home,
your wedding roses, ivory and crème, I buried my face
in the flowers of memory, inhaling deeply, remembering
an extravagance of roses in the Japanese garden,
garlands of white roses festooning the lucky red bridge,
pale petals floating on the winding stream, and roses
on your wedding dress, in tight buds, or open and opening.
Days of joy and grief . . . the minister advised, but we heard
    only *joy*,
the world full to overflowing with the day's promise.

That night a new moon rose, the hotel ablaze
on its high hill, its doors thrown open to the night.
Below, the city of angels burned bright, a mirror
to the burning stars above, and music swam in crests
and waves over darkened lawns and gardens.
Glasses raised to the sky, we offered the immemorial
toast, and I thought of words from an ancient time:
Dear to us ever, a poet wrote, *the banquet, harp, and dance,
and changes of raiment, and love, and sleep.*

Later, walking back through the Japanese garden,
I wondered, your window dark, did you love and sleep?
The sound of water running over stones was like the sound
of time itself, flowing and unstoppable. It was August.
Beside the path, the peach tree was heavy with peaches,
peaches scattered on the ground, the air sweet with abundance,
the delicate smell of peaches mingling, commingling,
like two lives, with the lingering scent of roses.

I Dreamed a Dream

On a dark summer night, I dreamed a dream:
I dreamed a moon, and the moon appeared,
lighting a house, a pond, a field.
And in the field, a white mare stood,
still center of the sleeping world.
I crossed dream's periphery into the field,
and mounting the mare we rode like the wind.
We rode as one to the silvered pond
where all was doubled in my dream.
Surrounded by stars, we drank our reflection,
lucky, I thought, and kept on dreaming.
I dreamed a woman, white as a bone,
slept alone in the house with the sheets
thrown off, her dream as cold as she was.
There, in the field, a peacock preened,
opening its rippling, many-eyed tail
(it made a sound like the wind when I rode)
to draw the moon closer, to make the moon love it.
But the moon was pitiless and would not be moved.
The peacock screamed at the cold, cold moon,
screamed with fury at the woman, too,
raking her face to make her scream.
Then it flew with a rush toward the moon
to rake, if it could, the moon's calm countenance,
its feathers falling into the field,
each eye staring upward, blind to the moon.
O helplessly drawn, I stepped into the field,
stepped deeper into the woman's dream,
to gather the tail into a seeing thing, thinking,
How beautiful are the eyes of heaven and hell.

I kneeled to gather sharp curving quills,
and there you were at the field's dark edge,
pale and unspeaking in clothes like the moon's,
caught in the crosswinds of two dreams,
the dream I dreamed, and the woman's.
All ended there as I walked toward you.
O love, I have told you everything.
Now in the common light of morning,
as we lie here caught by the sun,
tell me, if you know, why I dreamed what I did.

The Frame

The once-bright silver darkening. A frame
framing a gone likeness of you. Snow outside.
A coldness in the room. Your voice on the telephone,
lost and unsure. Words going back and forth,
and then a click, white silence filling up the line.
Alone, I slip you out of the frame to hold
and hold onto, light seeping through the sepia
tones to color the girl that you once were. On fire.
Your own proud creature. The world at heel.
A pride that carried you through tarnished years.
But Time would not stop for you and so you raged
at everything around you, *Betrayed*, you cried, *by all!*
                    But death is the great apologist.
It levels harsh landscapes, it softens the lines
in your face and changes the bitterness of memory
into something bittersweet, no longer gall.
The hard hills that you loved are now no more
than gently sloping mounds, rounded by falling snow.
And knowing what I know, I know that days unimaginable
wait. They wait for us. You will be mourned.

Like Water

It hadn't been three months since he had died
when we sat together in your living room,
a green world going on outside, the June wind
blowing hot and hard, bending each leaf and branch,
while inside all was still: a still interior where
three women sat in shadow stirring summer drinks,
the room the same as it had always been,

but changed, his absence palpable. You said,
"I thought I'd gradually miss him less, the way
a craving for a cigarette lessens a little after weeks
of going without. It's not like that." You paused,
drawing in a breath. "It's like a thirst that deepens
as each day passes. Like water," you finally said.
"I want him back the way I want a drink of water."

1999

In a hundred years, we won't be here,
replaced by the unimaginable, a flash,
a whir, as forests fall, rise up again,
and houses that we lived in disappear.
Changing our form, will we come back then?
Or stay underground, quiet and companionable?

Will poems be written then?
Whose hand will write them?
Will someone stand, time's ghost,
as I do now, in a peeling gazebo with antique
posts and scrollwork, here on the edge
of a lake, the edge of time so close?

To the west, the mountains are immovable,
a sheer cliff face that no one can climb.
Shadows play on the lake's surface
as clouds race by, seeded and shining,
a wind from the north whipping the water
into waves, unreadable to the eye.

In a hundred years, will the mountains
exhaust themselves? Will the lake move on?
Will my hand, severed from mind, lie fallow
forever? For a week or two, summer is endless.
Then we fall back into lives that rush forward
with terrible speed, our future glimpsed in dreams:

the gazebo gone, the dusty road paved over,
its blind curves straightened out, leading

nowhere we want to go, the sun and moon
whirling brightly above the figure of a tree,
its branches black as char, where no bird
sings and no wind blows through ever.

Once, all flesh and shadow, we prayed
for our own permanence. Now we stand
in the center of a vacancy that is the center
of the new, asking what will be left
when each thing goes. Our answer an echo:
The singing. Only the singing.

The Beautiful Day

A month after it happened, my daughter and I
stood in a rose garden a few miles

north of Baltimore. Espaliered pear and apple trees
climbed an old brick wall. It was a beautiful day,

but shadowed and deepened in a way
I could never have imagined before.

The sky was *intensely* blue, just like the day
                                        it happened.

Roses of every shade and hue
still bloomed, the first frost yet to come.

My daughter, nearly eleven, wished for a garden
like the one we stood in. A rose garden

surrounded by a curving wall.
Maybe someday . . . I said.

We stood there, watching weightless white spoors
of milkweed lift in the wind.

Uncountable numbers drifted upward and away,
each shining in the sun.

Like words. But what are words now?

Words are so small. Words have no weight.
And nothing will ever be the same.

September/October 2001

III

Her mother put her hand out, palm up, against the drizzle. "Maybe we get to be something like this rain when we die," she said. "We're there, but not really there. We'd be satisfied with just the smell of the chrysanthemums and the green tea. We wouldn't need much then."

— KYOKO MORI, *Shizuko's Daughter*

Above the Pagoda

In my next life, I will live in a house
with a roof that curls like a smile.
Outside, a script of trees and clouds.
Paths winding up the mountain.
Pilgrims climbing the ninety-nine steps
to the pagoda, carrying bright offerings.
Shivering, I will rise in the morning,
blow on my hands like coals,
and squat to make tea in the teapot.
Slowly, the tea will fill my heart
like a cup, the tea leaves swirling,
knowing more than I know.
In the room's far corner, an altar.
A few flowers, incense.
Buddha smiling.

How little will be necessary!
Like a beggar's bowl,
each day will be full and empty.
The white cherry dropping its petals.
A snail on a silent journey,
leaving a shining path.
The swollen moon floating in a pool,
disappearing, coming back.
A tipsy bee on the lip of the wine cup.
The sake overturned. Joy. Tears.
One life containing everything.

All will be a great wheel turning,
the seasons a pageant where

the low and the highborn parade
in rags and brilliant finery.
Such thoughts!
The years will pass.
My hair will fade to no color.
My face will be an old apple,
my eyes two moons when I smile.
Bent like a walking stick,
what will I think of then?
The past, captured and fixed forever?
The future, glimmering on the horizon?
In that far moment, will it seem
this life is no different from that one?

Two Characters in Search of a Metaphor

The characters may appear to be sitting or walking,
flying or moving, going away or coming back,
sad or happy, like Spring or Summer, Autumn or Winter,
like a bird pecking for food or an insect eating away wood,
like a sharp knife or dagger, or a strong bow and arrow,
like water and fire, like trees and clouds,
like the sun and moon following their course:
such is calligraphy.

—TS'AI YUNG (A. D. 133–192)

In the beginning, was it spring or summer?
Autumn or winter? Were we sad or happy?
Going or coming back? You were like fire,
I thought, and I was like water.
Or you were the fire, and I was the air,
quickly devoured. Some days I was a tree
spreading my arms, and you were a cloud
passing through me. Sometimes you were the tree,
snagging me on your bare black branches.
Apart, we were small, two figures on opposite
horizons, caught in a seasonless season.

We made our way in the world, like birds
leaving the nest, two hungry birds.
You were the sun, and I was the moon
going through my changes, following your course.
Like daggers in each other's pockets, our words
were shiny and dangerous, always flashing out.
As we walked and moved and flew, as we
passed the midpoint, as, restless, exhausted,

we went away and came back, did it matter
if we were sad or happy? Did we even know?

Like the sun and moon following their course,
the years kept passing, how many years?
You were the bow to my arrow,
or you were the unswerving arrow
aimed at the heart's moving target.
Like a quiet stream next to a campsite,
like dry kindling blazing into a bonfire,
or a tree's sudden flowering,
our lives kept changing, circling back.
Like the weather that is never one thing,
like words with more than one meaning:
that's how it was with us.

The Papermaker

Last year's poverty was not yet true poverty.
This year's poverty is at last true poverty.
Last year there was nowhere to place the gimlet.
This year the gimlet itself is gone.
—ZEN MONK HSIANG-YEN

In the hot heat of deep summer,
I dream of paper white as snow,
white winter paper,
drying in the hills.

The days repeat.
Each sheet is the first sheet,
alive, without ego, still,
until the poet speaks.

Here is the white field.
Here is the white field, waiting.
A black brush, a crow,
walks there, flies off.

What do I know?
The *I* disappearing
is the crow flying,
the clumsy crow.

Sweating, I wake,
holding nothing in my hands.
Again, I have dreamed
the dream of paper.

And what, you patiently ask,
is true poverty?
This sheet that I give you
upon which nothing is written.

Bruise

All black, a hard dark
spot, it sits in the tree's
bare arms. *Caw! Caw!*
it calls to no one.
Again, too rude: *Caw!*
The truth is out:
it eats dead things.
It knows that want
can make, unmake
a world as much as love,
love's awful opposite.
And so, once more,
the terrible syllable:
Caw! And then it lifts
its wings and flies
into a world diffuse,
green, and blameless,
leaving a bright spot
of nothing where it sat.
One oily feather
in slow free fall,
a bruised blue-black
iridescence,
is all that's left.
But still I hear it: *Caw!*
An ugly crow perched
in the charred chest
has left, knowing,
what does it know?
That the word

at the bottom of
the world is black.
I will not say it,
but pray that crow
not come back.

Silence

Brightness and flow, silence descends around me,
warm and dark as death. Shall I wear it like a mantle,
like a shroud that weighs me down heavily, this silence
that hollows out and fills the spaces of my body?

Shall I turn from light and life to name the other side?
This is the great silence in the middle of my life,
the place on the journey where the traveler halts,
exhausted, makes camp under the open sky,

not knowing if she'll wake. Here, in this place,
there are no names on the map. There is no map.
And the silence, like snow, effaces every road
and landmark, covers all that I am, all that I know.

What can I do but hold it close, close,
a small furred thing, savage even in repose,
that may be lulled to sleep, or may turn its fury,
tooth and claw, upon the living heart that spawned it?

Grass

I walked in the waist-high grass
where a million blades
sang in green cacophony.
Too many voices sang.
And in the din, I thought,
We are as grass,
as simple as grass,
our voices will be lost,
and all things pass . . .

I desired then
to be silent and alone,
like a stone spilled
by time into a field
the mower slowly
scythes, a stone
completely unto itself,
warmed by the sun,
shining in the sun.

Triptych for Three Tenses

1

You find me in every photograph,
gravely staring out at you,
whispering, *sotto voce*, "Remember . . . "
You try to walk away but can't.
Dear one, you must carry me,
carry me on your back.

2

You live for me but never meet me,
beseech me with "If only . . . "
I hear your refrain and am bored.
I have no face except the one you make,
hideous or lovely, as in a myth.
If you *did* see me, you'd be terrified.

3

Always I am *here*,
your tireless faithful companion,
and yet you fly in the face of reason
and prefer those other two.

Curio

Today, wave upon wave,
memories wash up
on the bracken-covered beach.

I walk the tide line,
picking and choosing,
making the worthless precious.

Stone, shell, carapace,
I put this one and that one
into my pocket.

What was ignored, passed over,
what nobody else wanted,
I will place among the curios,

discrete, exposed to
light's radiance. See how
they glimmer and shine.

Closer, come closer, and you
will smell the briny smell
of time, and sea, and rot.

That day, I will recall later,
laughing or weeping, brought
to my knees once more

by holy memory. *What once
was alive is dead, is alive
in memory* . . . I'll say to no one.

Wave upon wave, the memories
come. Nothing will stop them
until I, too, am a memory

to the ones that I loved.

Rocko

I often wondered who was walking who:
the old man in his red knit hat,
or his dog, a black Labrador retriever?

New to the block, I said hello one day
and stopped to pat the dog. *Rocko*,
the man told me, *his name is Rocko*.

He carried biscuits for the good Rocko
who knew a trick or two and did them
on command. Rocko was eleven then

which made him, as dog years go,
seventy-seven. Both man and dog
were slowing down. Bent crooked

as a cane, Rocko's master shuffled along
in sandals, his footsteps barely clearing
the cracked and heaving sidewalk

while Rocko skipped and limped from a bad hip.
Mornings and evenings, I watched unseen
from the window, thinking the unthinkable:

If Rocko died, who would walk the man?
I saw the old man, hatless, bereaved, wandering
without direction down a dim November street

where dead leaves swirled in little whirlwinds.
Or Rocko patiently waiting at the door,
his master cold on the floor, stopped

and still as a watch in need of winding.
O let them go on together forever, here,
or in a sunlit heaven we don't know

where paths are clear and level,
and it is always gentle spring or golden fall:
the brave old man and his good dog Rocko.

A Dream of Water

—We stood on a point surrounded on three sides by water.
Like an old looking glass, the bay wavered in the sun.
A wind came up, too strong for the day, blowing west to east,
breaking the bay into ten thousand pieces that all flowed out,
like running silver, leaving a mudflat. In an eyeblink,
grass and trees sprang up to make a green-gold meadow
where children played who took no notice of our gaze,
as if we were the apparitions, they flesh and blood,
and I thought, *Never will I see this happen again.*

I saw the moment passing as all moments pass,
but when I turned to you, the scene in your eyes, too,
it all changed back: the ocean rushing in to cover up
the meadow, the children gone, your eyes brimming
with the water of years held back too long.
Though all had vanished, I felt strange joy.
Above, gulls circled and laughed, circled and laughed,
the waves a series of small endless events, lapping
at thousands of smooth white stones on the shore,
the shining grey years of our lives before us.

"In Heaven It Is Always Autumn"

John Donne

In heaven it is always autumn. The leaves are always near
to falling there but never fall, and pairs of souls out walking
heaven's paths no longer feel the weight of years upon them.
Safe in heaven's calm, they take each other's arm,
the light shining through them, all joy and terror gone.
But we are far from heaven here, in a garden ragged and unkept
as Eden would be with the walls knocked down,
    the paths littered
with the unswept leaves of many years, bright keepsakes
for children of the Fall. The light is gold, the sun pulling
the long shadow soul out of each thing, disclosing an outcome.
The last roses of the year nod their frail heads,
like listeners listening to all that's said, to ask,
What brought us here? What seed? What rain? What light?
What forced us upward through dark earth? What made us bloom?
What wind shall take us soon, sweeping the garden bare?
Their voiceless voices hang there, as ours might,
if we were roses, too. Their beds are blanketed with leaves,
tended by an absent gardener whose life is elsewhere.
It is the last of many last days. Is it enough?
To rest in this moment? To turn our faces to the sun?
To watch the lineaments of a world passing?
To feel the metal of a black iron chair, cool and eternal,
press against our skin? To apprehend a chill as clouds
pass overhead, turning us to shivering shade and shadow?
And then to be restored, small miracle, the sun
    shining brightly
as before? We go on, you leading the way, a figure
leaning on a cane that leaves its mark on the earth.

My friend, you have led me farther than I have ever been.
To a garden in autumn. To a heaven of impermanence
where the final falling off is slow, a slow and radiant happening.
The light is gold. And while we're here, I think it must
  be heaven.

Notes and Dedications

"Dogwood" is in memory of Taghi Modarressi
"Flight Back": italicized lines are from Homer
"'In Heaven It Is Always Autumn'" is for Josephine Jacobsen

About the Author

Elizabeth Spires (b. 1952 in Lancaster, Ohio) is the author of four previous collections of poetry: *Globe, Swan's Island, Annonciade,* and *Worldling.* She also edited and introduced *The Instant of Knowing: Lectures, Criticism, and Occasional Prose of Josephine Jacobsen.*

Spires has been the recipient of a Whiting Award, a Guggenheim Fellowship, the Amy Lowell Travelling Poetry Scholarship, and two fellowships from the National Endowment for the Arts. In 1998 she received the Witter Bynner Prize for Poetry from the American Academy of Arts and Letters, and the Maryland Author Award from the Maryland Library Association. Her poems have been featured on National Public Radio and have appeared in *The New Yorker, Poetry, American Poetry Review, The New Criterion,* and in many anthologies.

Her books for children include *The Mouse of Amherst, I Am Arachne, With One White Wing,* and *Riddle Road.*

She lives in Baltimore with her husband, the novelist Madison Smartt Bell, and their daughter, Celia, and is a professor of English at Goucher College.